THE

A B C

BOOK

BJ Armstrong

Illustrated by BJ Armstrong

Lettering (except print "Gg, Hh, Ww, and Xx") by BJ Armstrong

Special Note: The picture for the letter "W" is a wigwam. This is also known as a
Teepee.

Printed in the United States of America

First Printing, 2015

ISBN 978-1-941749-42-5

4-P Publishing

Chattanooga, TN 37411

Publisher's Noe: The drawings and lettering were all created by BJ Armstrong in 1987.
There were salvaged from her collection after a fire. Any page discolorations you see are
not defects with printing. They are the results of smoke and water damage. 4-P publishing
decided to leave the marks as is because it give the coloring unique and authentic feel.

THE ABC BOOK

A B C D E F G
H I J K L M
N O P Q R S T
U V W X Y Z

a b c d e f g h i
j k l m n o p q r
s t u v w x y z

Objective:
  To teach the alphabet and words that begin with each manuscript letter.

1987

Aa

_ _ _ _ _

_ _ _ _

Bb

Cc

---- ----

Dd

---- ----

E e

_ _ _

F f

_ _ _ _ _

G g

H h

I i

J j

K k

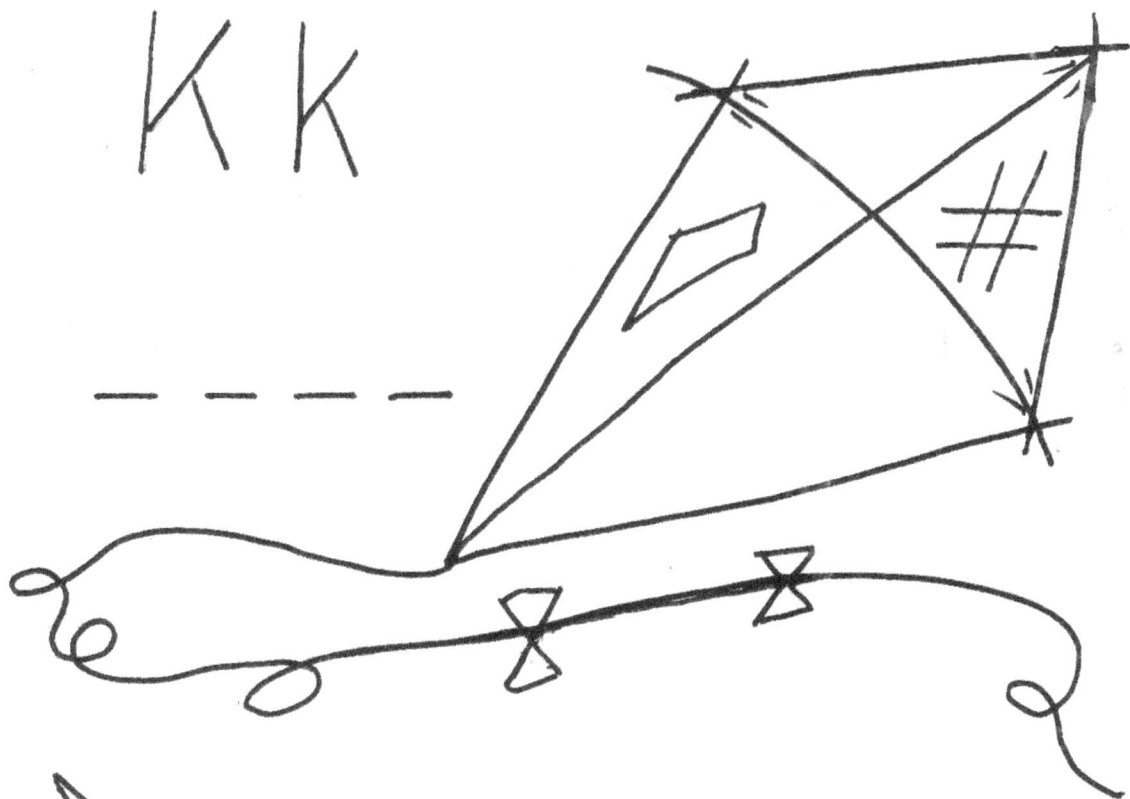

- - - - -

L l

- - - - -

M m

8   1   9   N n   10

            6

5   1   2   100

    4

3   0   _ _ _ _ _ _ _

O o

- - - - - -

P p

- - - - - - -

Q q

_ _ _ _ _

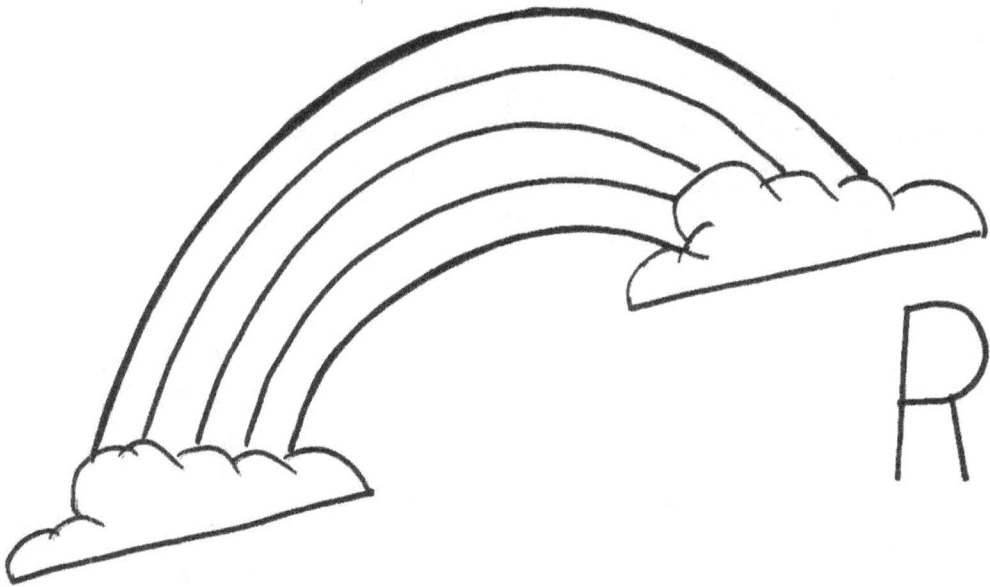

R r

_ _ _ _ _ _ _

S s

- - - - - - - -

T t

- - - - - -

U u

- - - - - - - - - -

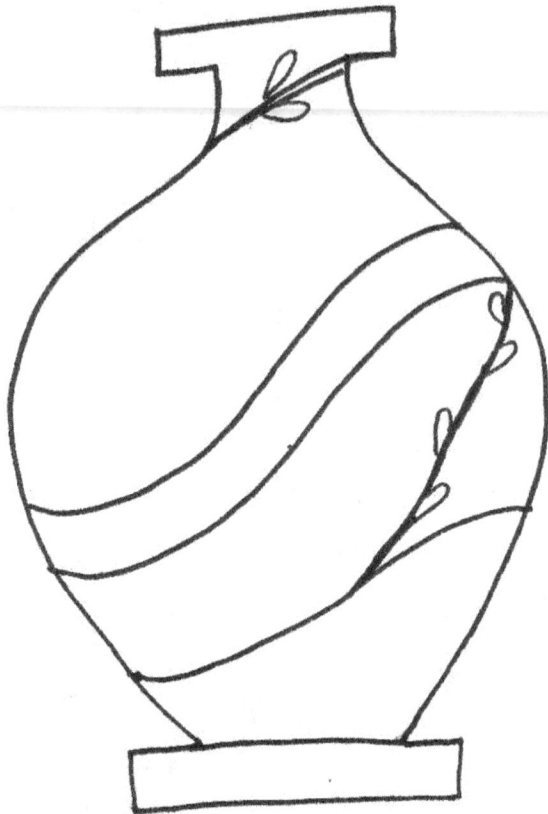

V v

- - - - -

W w

- - - -

- - - -

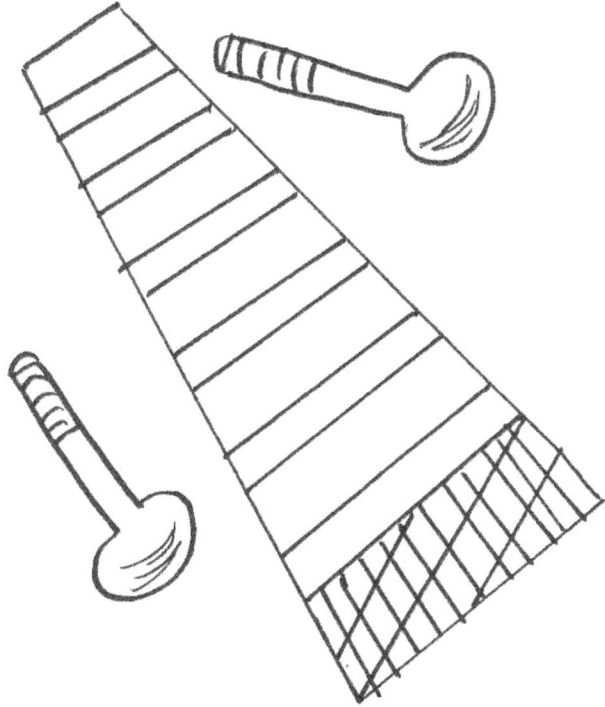

X x

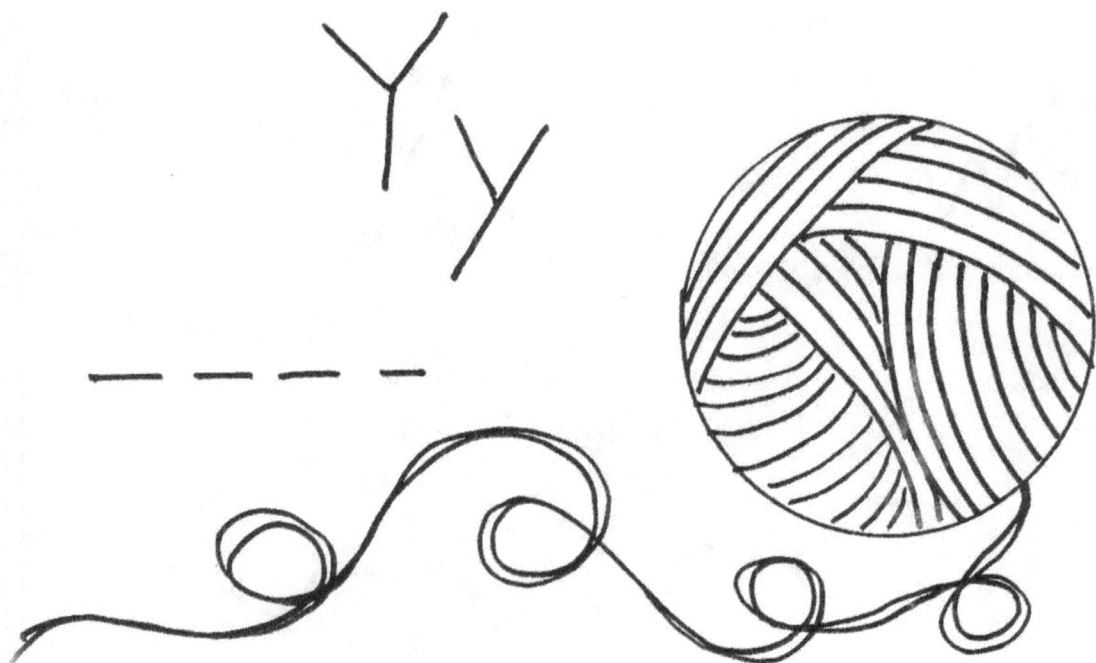

Y y

_ _ _ _ _

Z z

_ _ _ _ _

The A B C Book

A B C D E F G
H I J K L M
N O P Q R S T
U V W X Y Z

a b c d e f g h i j
k l m n o p q r
s t u v w x y z

Objective:
To teach the alphabet and words that begin with each cursive letter.

a a

_____

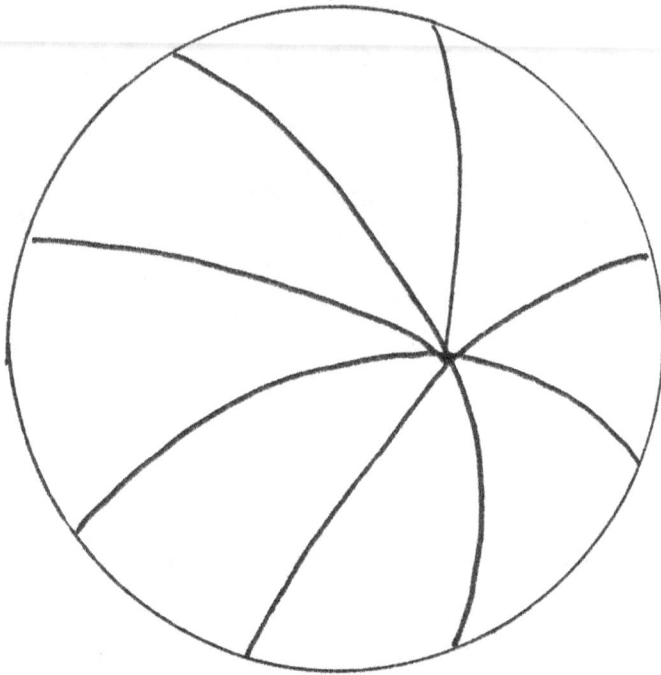

B b

_____

Cc

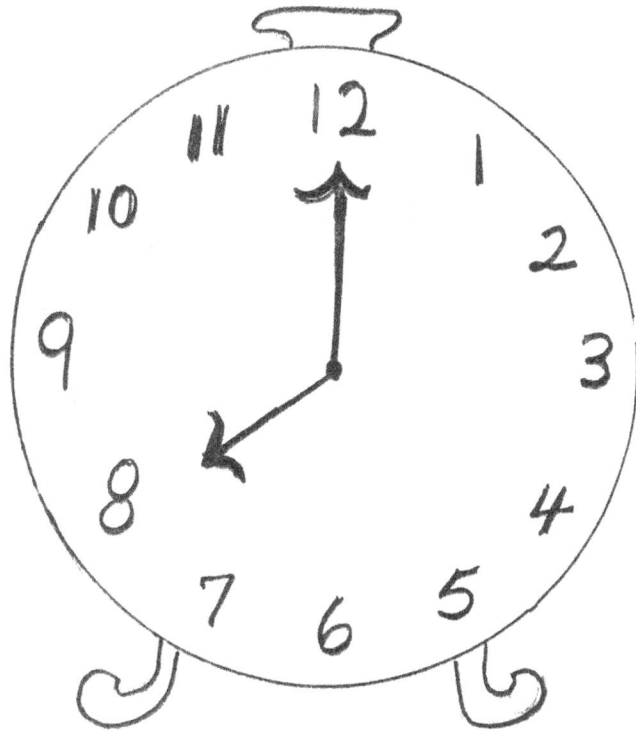

_____

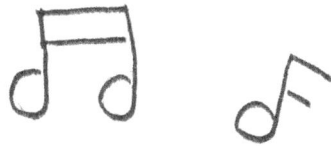

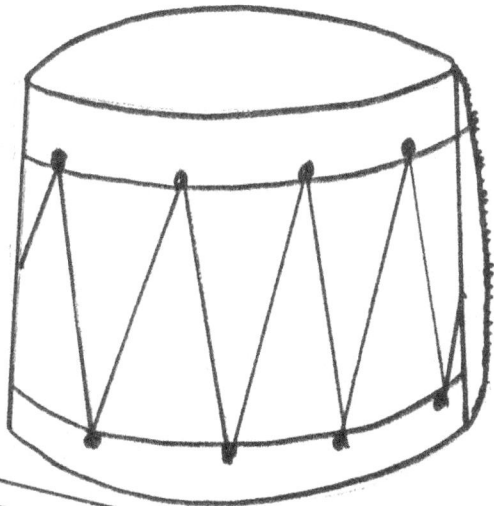

Dd

_____

Éé

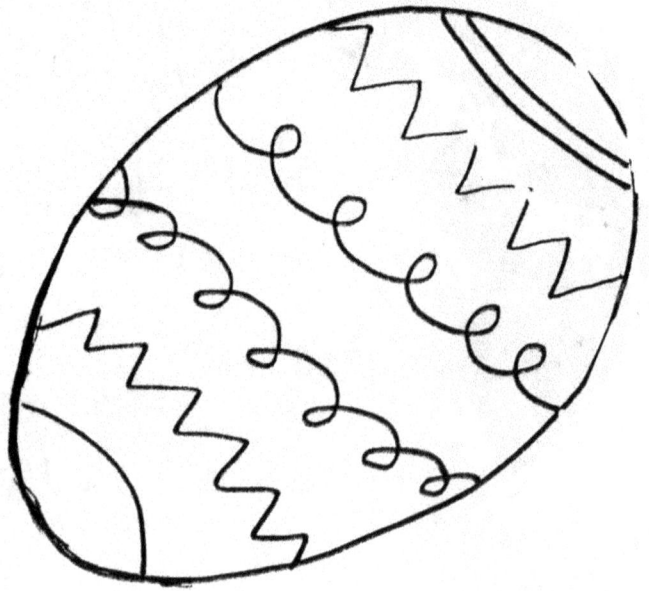

Ff

Gg

_____

Hh

_____

Ii

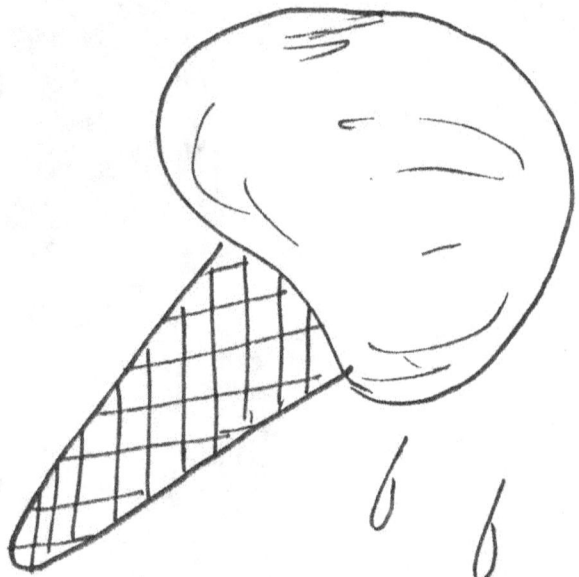

_____

_____

Jj

_____

_____

_____

$\mathcal{K}\,k$

_____

$\mathcal{L}\,l$

_____

M m

_____

Michael Jerome   N n

Bill   Betty

Jennifer _____

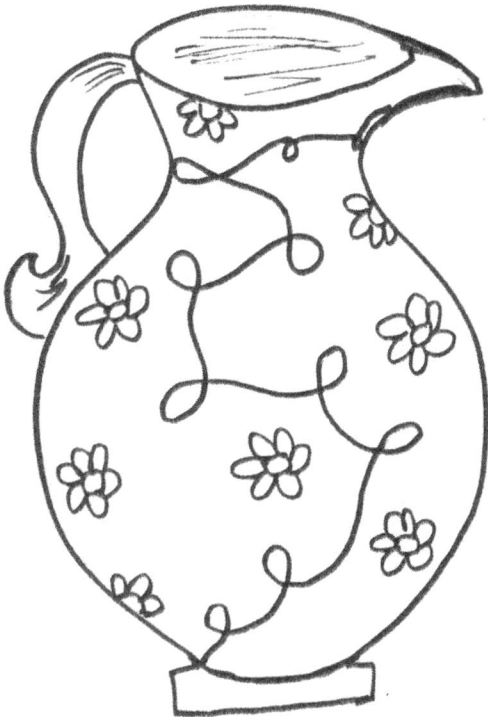

O o

_____

P p

_____

Qq

_____

Rr

_____

S s

_____

T t

_____

$\mathcal{U}u$

_____

LOVE

$\mathcal{V}v$

_____

W w

_____

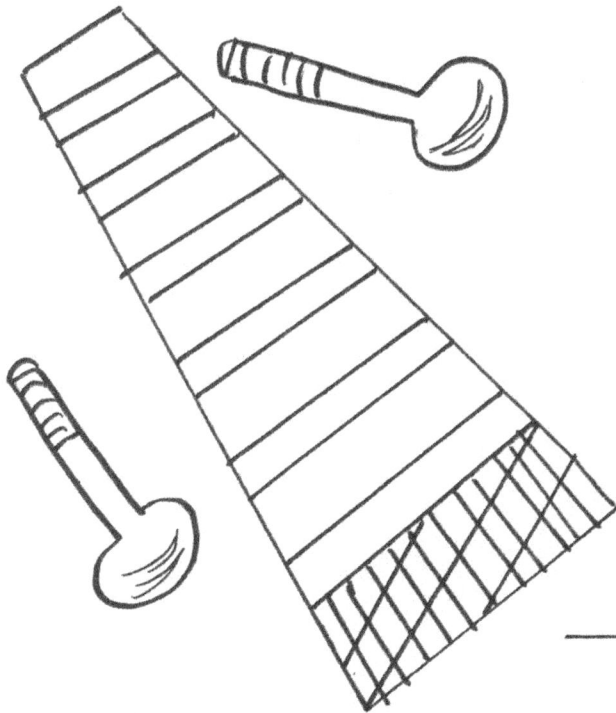

X x

_____

Y y

_____

Z z

_____

www.ingramcontent.com/pod-product-compliance
Lightning Source LLC
Chambersburg PA
CBHW080536030426
42337CB00023B/4764